Symphony No. 4
in E-flat Major, "Romantic"

Anton Bruckner

Edited by Robert Haas
for the International Bruckner Society

DOVER PUBLICATIONS, INC.
Mineola, New York

Copyright

Bibliographical Note

This Dover edition, first published in 2001, is an unabridged republication of the work originally published in *Anton Bruckner: Sämtliche Werke. Kritische Gesamtausgabe* by Bruckner-Verlag G.m.b.H., Leipzig, 1936, and appearing here in the form in which it was reprinted in 1952 by Vereinigung Volkseigener Verlage, Bruckner-Verlag. Lists of contents, instrumentation, and German terms are newly added. The introduction by Robert Haas appears here in a new English translation. The original editorial notes have been omitted.

International Standard Book Number: 0-486-41697-6

Manufactured in the United States of America
Dover Publications, Inc., 31 East 2nd Street, Mineola, N.Y. 11501

Contents

Symphony No. 4 in E-flat Major
"Romantic" (1874–80)

INSTRUMENTATION

2 Flutes [Flöten, Fl.]
2 Oboes [Oboen, Ob.]
2 Clarinets (B♭) [Klarinetten in B, Klar.]
2 Bassoons [Fagotte, Fag.]
4 Horns (F) [Hörner in F, Hrn.]
3 Trumpets (F) [Trompeten in F, Tromp.]
3 Trombones (Alto, Tenor, Bass) [Posaunen (A. T. B.), Pos.]
Tuba [Bass-Tuba, B.-Tuba]
Timpani [Pauken, Pk.]
Violins I, II [Violine, Viol.]
Violas [Vla.]
Cellos [Violoncell, Vc.]
Basses [Kontrabass, Kb.]

INTRODUCTION

The present score corresponds with Anton Bruckner's autograph, which he bequeathed in his will *as the final version* to Vienna's imperial Hofbibliothek and today is preserved as manuscript 19476 in the music collection of the Nationalbibliothek in Vienna. In it the first three movements of the second version of this symphony (1878) are combined with the Finale in its third version (1880).

The same four movements were engraved and published as early as November 1889 by the publishing house of Albert J. Gutmann in Vienna. This first edition of the score, however, departs conspicuously from the text that is here made accessible for the first time. The changes include, along with confusing additions of tempo indications and questionable dynamic revisions, a thoroughgoing reorchestration of the entire symphony and serious meddling with the form of the Scherzo and Finale. The most important examples of the last type are the disturbing of the balance in the first Scherzo through premature interruption (at m. 250) and the addition of a diminuendo transition, and, further, the elimination of the beginning of the recapitulation in the Finale, where 48 measures (mm. 383–430) were omitted. In the first edition the recapitulation begins with the cantabile passage in D minor (12 measures), while in the autograph it appears transposed to F♯ minor.

Although it is certain that the first edition appeared in the master's lifetime, the circumstances that accompanied its publication can today no longer be verified. The draft mentioned above, in any case, takes absolutely no notice of the text of the first edition, which under closer investigation turns out to be a murky source for the specialist—that is, the result of the conception of practitioners about Bruckner. This represented a point of view whose justification appears to have been grounded in the special, unfavorable circumstances of the time of the publication, when inadequately developed orchestral technique, possibilities of performances only with orchestras of the second rank, and in general the limited power of comprehension of the listener had to be taken into consideration, but which today has been superseded, since it gave a different meaning to the well-considered and significant intent of its creator and must have been accepted by Bruckner as, at best, an unavoidable expedient. (The more detailed discussions of the difficult question of the sources are found in the source commentary. [The latter has been omitted from the Dover volume.])

This volume of the complete-works edition thus does not contain the text of the first edition in its entirety; on the contrary, it provides the beautiful, unknown Finale of the second version of 1878 and the entire first version of the score of 1874. [*Note:* The Dover volume reproduces only the score as described in the first paragraph and published as an individual volume by the Bruckner-Verlag, that is, without the 1874 version of the symphony or the Finale of 1878.]

Vienna, February 1936 — Professor Robert Haas

In addition to the editor, Siegmund von Hausegger and Elsa Krüger participated in the redaction of the score.
Duration: approx. 1 hour.

Glossary of German Terms

anfangs, at the beginning
Anschwellung, crescendo

B, B-flat
bei, in
Besetzung, setting
bewegt, agitated, *bewegter,* more agitated
bis zum, until the
breit, broad, *breiter,* broader
Bruckners, Bruckner's (own)

das, the
der, the
deutlich, clearly
D. H., The Editor
die, the
doch, but

empfohlen, recommended
Es, E-flat
etwas, somewhat

feierlich, solemnly
fort u. fort, constantly

Gesangsperiode, songlike passage [mm. 93ff]
gesangvoll, songful, cantabile
gestrichen, bowed
geteilt, divisi
gezogen, drawn out, legato
gleicher, same

Hauptthema, main theme
hervortretend, prominent

im, in the
immer, always, becoming steadily
immer fort, immerfort, constantly
in, to, at

Jagdthema, hunting theme

keinesfalls, on no account
Klammern, parentheses

lang, long
länger, longer
langsam, slow, *langsamer,* slower

marcirt, markiert, emphatically, marcato
markig, emphatically, vigorously
mit, with

nach, (retunes) to
nicht, not
noch, still
Note, note

ohne, without

Partitur, score

recht, very
ruhig, peacefully, *ruhiger,* more peacefully

S., page
Saite, string
sanft, gently
schleppend, dragging
schnell, fast
schwer, heavily
sehr, very
selbst, himself
Spitze, tip of the bow
Spottvogel, mockingbird
Stärke, strength
steht, appears
Streicher, strings

Takt, measure
Teile, part
tief, low

u., und, and
über, over

vernehmbar, audibly
vgl., cf.
vier, four
Viertelnote, quarter-note

wie, as
wuchtig, vigorously, heavily

zu, too

1., 1tes, 1st
2te(s), 2nd
4tel, quarter

Symphony No. 4 in E-flat Major
"Romantic"
I

* (Klammern Bruckners)

20 30

hervortretend fort u. fort
1. Fl. 2.
mf
hervortretend fort u. fort
mf
hervortretend immer fort
1. in B Klar. 2. in B
mf
hervortretend immer fort
mf
Hrn. 1 in F
I.
p
divisi
Viol. 1
divisi
Viol. 2
divisi
Vla.
Vc.
Kb.

20 30

40

1. Fl. 2.
poco a poco cresc.
sempre cresc.
poco a poco cresc.
sempre cresc.
a 2
Ob. 1. 2
(mf cresc.)
sempre cresc.
1. in B Klar. 2. in B
poco a poco cresc.
sempre cresc.
poco a poco cresc.
sempre cresc.
cresc.
a 2
Hrn. 1. 2 in F
(I.)
mf cresc.
cresc. sempre
Viol. 1
poco a poco cresc.
sempre cresc.
Viol. 2
poco a poco cresc.
sempre cresc.
Vla.
poco a poco cresc.
sempre cresc.
Vc.
(mf) sempre cresc.

40

50
A
Fl. 1. 2.
a 2
Ob. 1. 2
Klar. 1. in B 2. in B
Fag. 1. 2
(a 2)
Hrn. 1. 2. in F 3. 4. in F
Tromp. 1. 2. in F 3. in F
Pos. A. T. B.
B.-Tuba
Pk.
Viol. 1
Viol. 2
Vla.
Vc.
Kb.
molto cresc.
(molto cresc.)
ff
marc.
ff marc.
I.
II.
(ff)
50
A

60
1.
Fl.
2.
Ob.1.2
1. in B
Klar.
2. in B
(a 2)
Fag.1.2
a 2
1.2. in F
Hrn.
3.4. in F
marc. sempre
1.2.inF
Tromp.
3. inF
mf
f
A.T.
Pos.
B.
B.-Tuba
Pk.
Viol.1
Viol.2
Vla.
Vc.
gezogen
Kb.
gezogen
60

70
Fl.
1.
2.
(a 2)
Ob. 1.2
Klar.
1. in B
2. in B
Fag. 1.2
Hrn.
1.2. in F
3.4. in F
Tromp.
1.2. in F
3. in F
marc.
Pos.
A. T.
B.
B.-Tuba
Viol. 1
Viol. 2
Vla.
Vc.
Kb.
70

1.
Fl.
2.
(a 2)
Ob. 1.2
1. in B
Klar.
2. in B
Fag. 1.2
a 2
1.2. in F
Hrn.
3.4. in F
II.
I.
p
1.2. in F
Tromp.
3. in F
A. T.
Pos.
B.
B.-Tuba
B
Viol. 1
spicc.
p hervortretend
spicc.
hervortretend
Viol. 2
p
deutlich hervortretend
Vla.
p
Vc.
p
pizz.
Kb.
B (p)

80
1.
Fl.
2.
Ob. 1
I.
1. in B
Klar.
2. in B
Fag. 1.
I.
1.2. in F
Hrn.
3.4. in F
Tromp. 1 in F
A. T.
Pos.
B.
Viol. 1
spicc.
Viol. 2
cresc.
Vla.
pizz.
arco
Vc.
Kb.
80

90
Fl.
1.
2.
a 2
Ob. 1. 2
Klar.
1. in B
2. in B
Fag. 1
I.
Hrn.
1.2. in F
I.
II.
3.4. in F
Tromp. 1 in F
I.
Pos.
A. T.
B.
Viol. 1
Viol. 2
Vla.
Vc.
Kb.
arco
pizz.
dim.
90

C
100
1. Fl. 2.
1. in B Klar. 2. in B
1.2. in F Hrn. 3.4. in F
A. T. Pos. B.
Viol. 1
Viol. 2
Vla.
Vc.
Kb.
pp
p
mf
I.
spicc.
mf hervortretend
lang gezogen
Ob. 1
(p)
Hrn. 3.4 in F
cresc.
divisi
tr
gezogen
dimin.
I. (= III.)

Klar.1 in B
Hrn.3 in F
Viol.1
Viol.2
Vla.
Vc.
Kb.
I.
110
spicc.
poco a poco cresc.
1. Fl. 2.
Ob.1.2
1. in B Klar. 2. in B
Fag.1.2
1.2. in F Hrn. 3.4. in F
1.2. in F Tromp. 3. in F
A. T. Pos. B.
B.-Tuba
Pk.
mf cresc. sempre
D
120
a 2
ff
ff marc.
f cresc.
cresc.
(a 2)
arco

1.
Fl.
2.
a 2
Ob.1.2
1. in B
Klar.
2. in B
a 2
Fag.1.2
(a 2)
1.2. in F
Hrn.
3.4. in F
(a 2)
marc.
1.2. in F
Tromp.
3. in F
(a 2)
A. T.
Pos.
B.
(a 2)
B.-Tuba
Pk.
Viol. 1
Viol. 2
Vla.
Vc.
Kb.

130
1.
Fl.
2
(a 2)
Ob.1.2
I.
mf
1.in B
Klar.
2.in B
mf
Fag.1.2
1.2.in F
Hrn.
3.4.in F
(a 2)
1.2.in F
Tromp.
3.in F
A.T.
Pos.
B.
B.-Tuba
Pk.
Viol.1
ppp
Viol.2
Vla.
divisi
Vc.
Kb.
130

1.
Fl.
2.
Ob.1.2
1.in B
Klar.
2.in B
Fag.1.2
1.2.in F
Hrn.
3.4.in F
1.2.in F
Tromp.
3.in F
A.T.
Pos.
B.
B.-Tuba
Viol.1
Viol.2
Vla.
Vc.
Kb.
mf cresc.
f cresc. sempre
a 2
poco a poco crescendo

140
E
1.
Fl.
2.
Ob.1.2
1.in B
Klar.
2.in B
Fag.1.2
(a 2)
1.2.in F
Hrn.
3.4.in F
1.2.in F
Tromp.
3.in F
a 2
ff marc. sempre
A.T.
Pos.
B.
B.-Tuba
Viol.1
Viol.2
Vla.
Vc.
Kb.

150
1.
Fl.
2.
Ob.1.2
a 2
p
1.in B
Klar.
2.in B
Fag.1.2
1.2.in F
Hrn.
3.4.in F
(a 2)
1.2.in F
Tromp.
3.in F
A.T.
Pos.
B.
B.-Tuba
Viol.1
Viol.2
Vla.
Vc.
Kb.
lang gezogen
trem. sempre
tremul. sempre
dimin.
ppp
pp
150

160
1.
Fl.
2.
Ob.1.2
(a 2)
1.in B
Klar.
2.in B
Fag.1.2
1.2.in F
Hrn.
3.4.in F
1.2.in F
Tromp.
3.in F
A.T.
Pos.
B.
B.-Tuba
Viol.1
Viol.2
Vla.
Vc.
Kb.
p poco a poco cresc.
cresc. sempre
f cresc.
a 2
poco a poco crescendo
sempre cresc.
160

F
170
1.
Fl.
2.
(a 2)
Ob.1.2
1.in B
Klar.
2.in B
(a 2)
Fag.1.2
(a 2)
1.2.in F
Hrn.
(a 2)
3.4.in F
ff marc.
1.2.in F
Tromp.
3.in F
A.T.
Pos.
B.
B.-Tuba
Viol.1
Viol.2
Vla.
Vc.
Kb.
ff
pp
ppp

180
a 2
Ob.1.2
1. in B
Klar.
2. in B
Fag.1.2
Hrn.1
in F
I.
Pk.
Viol.1
Viol.2
Vla.
Vc.
Kb.
mf
p
pp
ppp
ppp sempre
190
(ppp)

G
200
Ob.1
Klar.1
in B
Pk.
Viol.1
Viol.2
Vla.
Vc.
Kb.
I.
pp
sempre ppp
ppp sempre
pizz.
210
Fl.1
p
ppp
(arco)

H
220
Fl. 1
Klar. 1 in B
Hrn. 1 in F
Viol. 1
Viol. 2
Vla.
Vc.
Kb.
I.
p
dimin.
pp
(pp)
cresc.
Ob. 1
Fag. 1
230
mf
dim.
dimin.
ppp
I. Solo
p sanft hervortretend immer fort

240
1.
Fl.
2.
Ob.1.2
1.in B
Klar.
2.in B
Hrn 1.2
in F
Viol.1
Viol.2
Vla.
Vc.
I.
mf
p
p poco a poco cresc.
(p) cresc.
dim.
a 2
cresc.
pp
poco a poco cresc.
p cresc.
cresc. sempre
(a 2)
1.2.in F
Hrn.
3.4.in F
crescendo sempre
mf cresc. sempre
A. T.
Pos.
B.
f (cresc. sempre)
Pk.

250
1. Fl. 2.
Ob. 1. 2
1. in B Klar. 2. in B
Fag. 1. 2
1. 2. in F Hrn. 3. 4. in F
1. 2. in F Tromp. 3. in F
A. T. Pos. B.
B.-Tuba
Pk.
Viol. 1
Viol. 2
Vla.
Vc.
Kb.
I
(a 2)
a 2
fff sempre marc.
fff marc. sempre
fff
250

260
1.
Fl.
2.
Ob. 1. 2
(a 2)
1. in B
Klar.
2. in B
Fag. 1. 2
a 2
1. 2. in F
Hrn.
3. 4. in F
(a 2)
1. 2. in F
Tromp.
3. in F
A. T.
Pos.
B.
B.-Tuba
Pk.
Viol. 1
Viol. 2
Vla.
Vc.
Kb.
260

270
1.
Fl.
2.
(a 2)
Ob. 1. 2
1. in B
Klar.
2. in B
(a 2)
Fag. 1. 2
(a 2)
1. 2. in F
Hrn.
3. 4. in F
1. 2. in F
Tromp.
3. in F
(a 2)
A. T.
Pos.
B.
B.-Tuba
8
loco
Viol. 1
Viol. 2
Vla.
Vc.
Kb.
p
pp
270

1.
Fl.
2.
Ob. 1. 2
(a 2)
1. in B
Klar.
2. in B
Fag. 1. 2
1. 2. in F
Hrn.
3. 4. in F
1. 2. in F
Tromp.
3. in F
A. T.
Pos.
B.
B.-Tuba
Viol. 1
Viol. 2
Vla.
Vc.
Kb.
mf
f
(poco a poco cresc.)
fff
cresc.
mf poco a poco cresc.
a 2
mf poco a poco crescendo
mf poco a poco cresc.

280
K
1.
Fl.
2.
(a 2)
Ob. 1.2
1. in B
Klar.
2. in B
Fag. 1.2
a 2
1.2. in F
Hrn.
3.4. in F
1.2. in F
Tromp.
3. in F
A. T.
Pos.
B.
B.-Tuba
Viol. 1
pp
Viol. 2
Vla.
Vc.
Kb.

290
300
Fl. 1
Ob. 1
Klar. 1. in B
Hrn. 1. 2 in F
Viol. 1
Viol. 2
Vla.
I.
p
cresc.
a 2
marc.
mf sanft hervortretend
f cresc.
p cresc.
mf cresc.
mf lang gezogen
310
1. in B
Klar.
2. in B
Fag. 1. 2
(a 2)
1. 2. in F
Hrn.
3. 4. in F
Tromp.
3. in F
A. T.
Pos.
B.
B.-Tuba
ff
lang gezogen immer

320
1. in B
Klar.
2. in B
(a 2)
Fag. 1.2
1.2 in F
Hrn.
3.4 in F
1.2. in F
Tromp.
3. in F
A. T.
Pos.
B.
B.-Tuba
Viol. 1
Viol. 2
Vla.
320
330
1. in B
Klar.
2. in B
(a 2)
Fag. 1.2
1.2. in F
Hrn.
3.4. in F
dimin. sempre
dim. sempre
1.2. in F
Tromp.
3 in F
I.
f
mf
A. T.
Pos.
B.
dim. sempre
dim. sempre
B.-Tuba
dim. sempre
Viol. 1
dim.
Viol. 2
dim.
Vla.
330

L
340
1. 2. in F
Hrn.
3. 4. in F
A. T.
Pos.
B.
B.-Tuba
Viol. 1
Viol. 2
Vla.
Vc.
Kb.
pp
pp lang gezogen immer
lang gezogen
divisi
lang
350
Fl. 1
Pk.
I.
p
ppp
cresc.
immer lang gezogen
gezogen
dim.
ppp

360
M
I.
ppp
p
Fl. 1
I. Solo
1. in F
Hrn.
3. in F
mf immer deutlich hervortretend
I.(=III.)
mf immer deutlich hervortretend
Pk.
p hervortretend
trem.
Viol. 1
ppp
Viol. 2
Vla.
Vc.
Kb.
370
p
divisi

380
390
1
Fl.
2
Ob.1.2
1. in B
Klar.
2. in B
Hrn.
1 in F
Pk.
Viol.1
Viol.2
Vla.
Vc.
Kb.
mf immer hervortretend
a 2
I.
p
divisi
400
(a 2)
(I.)
1.2. in F
3.4. in F
poco a poco cresc.
cresc.
p cresc.
gezogen
(poco a poco cresc.)

410
1. Fl. 2.
p
Ob. 1.2
a 2
1. in B Klar. 2. in B
Fag. 1.2
1.2. in F Hrn. 3.4. in F
(a 2)
I.
pp
1.2. in F Tromp. 3. in F
A. T. Pos. B.
B.-Tuba
Pk.
Viol. 1
pp sempre
Viol. 2
pp sempre
(divisi)
Vla.
pp sempre
Vc.
pp sempre
Kb.
410

N
420
1.
Fl.
2.
Ob.1.2
1. in B
Klar.
2. in B
Fag.1.2
a 2
1.2. in F
Hrn.
3.4. in F
marc. sempre
1.2. in F
Tromp.
3. in F
marc.
A.T.
Pos.
B.
ff marc.
B.-Tuba
Pk.
Viol.1
Viol.2
Vla.
Vc.
Kb.

1.
Fl.
2.
Ob. 1.2
1. in B
Klar.
2. in B
Fag. 1.2
1.2. in F
Hrn.
3.4. in F
1.2. in F
Tromp.
3. in F
A.T.
Pos.
B.
B.-Tuba
Pk.
Viol. 1
Viol. 2
Vla.
Vc.
Kb.
marc.
gezogen

430
1. Fl. 2.
Ob. 1.2
1. in B Klar. 2. in B
Fag. 1.2
a 2
1.2. in F Hrn. 3.4. in F
1.2. in F Tromp. 3. in F
A. T. Pos. B.
B.-Tuba
Pk.
Viol. 1
Viol. 2
Vla.
Vc.
Kb.
I.
p
mf hervortretend
pizz.
430
440
1. in B Klar. 2. in B
Viol. 1
Viol. 2
Vla.
Vc.
Kb.
pp
ppp
440

450
1.
Fl.
2.
Ob. 1.2
a 2
1. in B
Klar.
2. in B
Fag. 1.2
1.2. in F
Hrn.
3.4. in F
I.
1.2. in F
Tromp.
3. in F
A. T.
Pos.
B.
lang gezogen
Viol. 1
spicc.
Viol. 2
Vla.
divisi
Vc.
arco
Kb.
450

1.
Fl.
2.
(a 2)
Ob. 1.2
1. in B
Klar.
2. in B
(a 2)
Fag. 1.2
1.2. in F
Hrn.
3.4. in F
1.2. in F
Tromp.
3. in F
A. T.
Pos.
B.
Viol. 1
Viol. 2
Vla.
Vc.
Kb.

460
1.
Fl.
2.
(a 2)
Ob. 1. 2
II. pp
1. in B
Klar.
2. in B
II.
Fag 1. 2
I.
1. 2. in F
Hrn.
3. 4. in F
1. 2. in F
Tromp.
3. in F
A. T.
Pos.
B.
Viol. 1
dimin.
spicc.
Viol. 2
Vla.
lang gezogen
Vc.
mf hervortretend
pizz.
Kb.
460

1.
Fl.
2.
p
cresc.
Ob. 1.2
I.
II.
pp
1.in B
Klar.
2.in B
Hrn.
3.4 in F
Tromp.
1 in F
pp
A.T.
Pos.
B.
Viol. 1
Viol. 2
pizz.
arco
divisi
ppp
pp sanft
Vla.
Vc.
gezogen
dimin.
Kb.
470
Fl. 1
Ob. 1. 2
a 2
Hrn.
1 in F
Pk.
hervortretend
470

480
1.
Fl.
2.
Ob. 1. 2
(a 2)
cresc.
1. in B
Klar.
2. in B
Fag. 1. 2
1. 2. in F
Hrn.
3. 4. in F
1. 2. in F
Tromp.
3. in F
A. T.
Pos.
B.
B.-Tuba
Pk.
Viol. 1
Viol. 2
Vla.
Vc.
Kb.
mf sempre cresc.
a 2 marc. sempre
marc. sempre
mf sempre cresc. et marc.
crescendo
mf (cresc.)
mf (sempre cresc.)
480

Q
ff sempre
490
1.
Fl.
2.
Ob.1.2
a 2
1. in B
Klar
2. in B
Fag.1.2
1.2. in F
Hrn.
3.4. in F
ff marc.
Tromp.
3. in F
ff (marc.)
A.T.
Pos.
B.
B.-Tuba
Pk.
ff
Viol.1
Viol.2
Vla.
Vc.
Kb.

1.
Fl.
2.
(a 2)
Ob. 1. 2
1. in B
Klar.
2. in B
Fag. 1. 2
1. 2. in F
Hrn.
3. 4. in F
1. 2. in F
Tromp.
3. in F
A. T.
Pos.
B
B.-Tuba
Viol. 1
Viol. 2
Vla.
Vc.
Kb.
dimin. sempre
dim. sempre
dimin. sempre
dimin. sempre
dimin. sempre
500
Klar. 1
in B
Hrn. 1
in F
Viol. 1
Viol. 2
Vla.
Vc.
Kb.
I.
p
I.
pp
pp
pp
pp
pp gezogen
pp gezogen
ppp
ppp
ppp
ppp
ppp
500

Fl. 1
Ob. 1
Klar. 1 in B
Fag. 1. 2
Hrn. 1 in F
Tromp. 1 in F
A. T.
Pos.
B.
Viol. 1
Viol. 2
Vla.
Vc.
Kb.
cresc.
p dim.
510
Fag. 2
1. 2. in F
Hrn.
3. 4. in F
1. 2. in F
Tromp.
3. in F

520
R
1.
Fl.
2.
a 2
Ob. 1. 2
1. in B
Klar.
2. in B
Fag. 1. 2
a 2
1. 2. in F
Hrn.
(a 2)
3. 4. in F
1. 2. in F
Tromp.
3. in F
A. T.
Pos.
B.
B.-Tuba
lang gezogen
Viol. 1
Viol. 2
Vla.
Vc.
Kb.
520
Klar. 1 in B
I.
pp
Fag. 1
Viol. 1
pp dimin.
ppp
Viol. 2
Vla.
Vc.
Kb.

530
S
I.
Ob. 1
Klar. 1
in B
Fag. 1
Hrn. 3
in F
I. (= III.)
A. T.
Pos.
B.
Viol. 1
Viol. 2
Vla.
(divisi)
Vc.
Kb.
530
540
1.
Fl.
2.
Ob. 1. 2
I.
Klar. 1
in B
1. 2. in F
Hrn.
3. in F
(III.)
A. T.
Pos.
B.
Viol. 1
Viol. 2
Vla
Vc.
Kb.
540

1.
Fl.
2.
Ob. 1.2
1. in B
Klar.
2. in B
Fag. 1. 2
1.2. in F
Hrn.
3.4. in F
I. (=III)
(IV.)
1.2. in F
Tromp.
3. in F
A. T.
Pos.
B.
B.-Tuba
Pk.
Viol. 1
Viol. 2
Vla.
Vc.
Kb.
poco a poco cresc.
p poco a poco cresc.
pp
p cresc.
poco a poco crescendo

550
1.
Fl.
2.
Ob. 1. 2
1. in B
Klar.
2. in B
Fag. 1. 2
1. 2. in F
Hrn.
3. 4. in F
a 2
1. 2. in F
Tromp.
3. in F
A. T.
Pos.
B.
B.-Tuba
Pk.
Viol. 1
Viol. 2
Vla.
Vc.
Kb.
cresc. semp.
mf
cresc. sempre
550

1.
Fl.
2.
Ob.1.2
1. in B
Klar.
2. in B
Fag.1.2
1.2. in F
Hrn.
3.4. in F
1.2. in F
Tromp.
3. in F
A.T.
Pos.
B.
B.-Tuba
Pk.
Viol.1
Viol.2
Vla.
Vc.
Kb.
marc. semp.
marc. sempre
(cresc.)
f marc. semp.
a 2
(a 2)
ff
ff gezogen

560
1.
Fl.
2.
Ob. 1.2
1. in B
Klar.
2. in B
Fag. 1.2
(a 2)
1.2. in F
Hrn.
(a 2)
3.4. in F
1.2. in F
Tromp.
3. in F
A.T.
Pos.
B.
B.-Tuba
Pk.
Viol. 1
Viol. 2
Vla.
Vc.
Kb.
560

570
1.
Fl.
2.
Ob. 1. 2
1. in B
Klar.
2. in B
Fag. 1. 2
(a 2)
1. 2. in F
Hrn.
3. 4 in F
(a 2)
(a 2)
1. 2. in F
Tromp.
3. in F
A. T.
Pos.
B.
B.-Tuba
Pk.
Viol. 1
Viol. 2
Vla.
Vc.
Kb.
570

II: ANDANTE

Andante quasi Allegretto
1.
Flöten
2.
Oboen 1. 2
1. in B
Klarinetten
2. in B
Fagotte 1. 2
1. 2. in F
Hörner
3. 4. in F
I.
p
1. 2. in F
Trompeten
3. in F
Alt, Tenor
Posaunen
Baß
Baß-Tuba
Pauken
C-G
(Andante quasi Allegretto)
con Sordini
Violine 1
pp
con Sordini
Violine 2
pp
con Sordini
Viola
pp
lang gezogen
Violoncell
mf immer deutlich hervortretend
Kontrabaß
(Andante quasi Allegretto)

10
Hrn. 1 in F
I.
pp
Viol.1
cresc.
ppp
pizz.
Viol.2
cresc.
dim.
ppp
pizz.
Vla.
cresc.
dim.
ppp gezogen
pizz.
Vc.
cresc.
dim.
ppp gezogen
pizz.
10
A
1.
Fl.
2.
mf
cresc.
Ob. 1.2
a 2
mf
cresc.
1. in B
Klar.
2. in B
mf
cresc.
Hrn. 1 in F
I.
p
Tromp. 1.2 in F
pp
A
arco
Viol.1
pp
crescendo
pp
Viol.2
arco
pp
crescendo
pp
Vla.
arco
pp
cresc.
pp
arco
Vc.
pizz.
pp
cresc.
pp
Kb.
pizz.
pp
crescendo
A

20
1.2. in F
Hrn.
3.4. in F
Viol. 1
Viol. 2
Vla.
Vc.
Kb.
pizz.
dimin.
ppp
arco
lang gezogen
crescendo sempre
(crescendo)
divisi
B
30
1.
Fl.
2.
1. in B
Klar.
2. in B
Hrn.
1 in F
A. T.
Pos.
B.
cresc.

40
1.
Fl.
2.
ff
dimin.
Ob. 1. 2
a 2
f
p
1. in B
Klar.
2. in B
dimin
Fag. 1
I.
Hrn.
1. 2. in F
(I.)
(II.)
A. T.
Pos.
B.
Pk.
pp
ppp
Viol. 1
cresc.
Viol. 2
Vla.
Vc.
Kb.
50
C
1. 2. in F
Hrn.
3. 4. in F
pizz.
lang gezogen
arco
gezogen
mf
dim.
cresc.
crescendo

60
Viol. 1
Viol. 2
Vla.
Vc.
pp
crescendo
cresc.
dim.
dimin.
gezogen
Hrn. 1 in F
I.
p
D
ppp
lang gezogen
mf
divisi
pizz.
Kb.
70
f
cresc.
mf gezogen
80
p legato sempre

I.
Fl. 1
pp
Ob. 1.2
p
dim.
1. in B
Klar.
2. in B
Fag. 1
Hrn.
1. in F
3. in F
dimin.
(III.)
Viol. 1
Viol. 2
Vla.
Vc.
90
Fl.
ppp
(I.)
Fag. 1.2
a 2
mf
f
1.2. in F
3.4. in F
I. (= III.)
arco
lang gezogen
markig
(divisi)
divisi
cresc.
(cresc.)
hervortretend
Kb.

100
E
1.
Fl.
2.
Ob. 1
1. in B
Klar.
2. in B
(a 2)
Fag. 1.2
Hrn.
1.2 in F
hervortretend
Tromp.
1 in F
I.
mf hervortretend
A. T.
Pos.
B.
Viol. 1
sine Sordini
mf markig
arco
cresc.
dimin.
Viol. 2
sine Sordini
mf markig
pizz.
Vla.
sine Sord.
mf markig
arco
mf lang gezogen
Vc.
mf markig
pizz.
Kb.
pizz.
100
E
Ob. 1.2
a 2
f hervortretend
Hrn.
1 in F
I.
mf hervortretend

F
110
1. Fl. 2.
(a 2)
Ob. 1.2
1. in B Klar. 2. in B
Fag. 1.2
a 2
(I.)
1.2. in F Hrn. 3.4. in F
a 2
1.2. in F Tromp. 3. in F
A. T. Pos. B.
spiccato
Viol. 1
Viol. 2
arco
Vla.
lang gezogen
Vc.
marcato gestrichen
Kb.

1.
Fl.
2.
Ob. 1.2
a 2
1. in B
Klar.
2. in B
Fag. 1.2
(a 2)
1. 2. in F
Hrn.
3. 4. in F
(a 2)
II. (= IV.)
1. 2. in F
Tromp.
3. in F
a 2
A. T.
Pos.
B.
Viol. 1
Viol. 2
Vla.
(divisi)
Vc.
Kb.
ff

1.
Fl.
2.
(a 2)
Ob. 1.2
1. in B
Klar.
2. in B
(a 2)
Fag. 1.2
(a 2)
1.2. in F
Hrn.
3.4. in F
dimin.
I.
pp
dimin.
pp
a 2
1.2. in F
Tromp.
3. in F
A. T.
Pos.
B.
pp
pp
Viol. 1
dimin.
pp
Viol. 2
dimin.
pp
Vla.
dimin.
pp
Vc.
lang gezogen
dimin.
pp
Kb.
lang gezogen
dimin.
pp

120
1.2. in F
Hrn.
3.4. in F
II. (=IV.) dimin.
A. T.
Pos.
B.
Pk.
Viol. 1
Viol. 2
Vla.
Vc.
Kb.
G
130
Fl. 1
Ob. 1
con Sordini
lang gezogen
mf immer deutlich hervortretend
cresc.
dimin.

H
140
Fl. 1
Ob. 1
1. in B
Klar.
2. in B
1. 2. in F
Hrn.
3. 4. in F
Viol. 1
Viol. 2
Vla.
Vc.
Kb.
pp
I.
G Saite
arco
pizz.
ppp
p lang gezogen
(divisi)
ppp gezogen
Ob. 1
1. in B
Klar.
2. in B
1. 2. in F
Hrn.
3. in F
Tromp. 1
in F
Viol. 1
Viol. 2
Vla.
Vc.
Kb.
mf
dim.
pp dimin.
poco a poco cresc.
arco
p poco a poco cresc.
p poco a poco crescendo
dimin.
lang gezogen

Fl. 1
Ob. 1
Klar. 1 in B
1. 2. in F
Hrn.
3. in F
Viol. 1
Viol. 2
Vla.
Vc.
Kb.
Hrn. 1 in F
150
160
I.
II.
con Sordino
(pp) dimin.
p dimin.
pizz.
arco
lang gezogen
gezogen
cresc.
dim.
crescendo
(crescendo)
dimin.
(sine Sordino)
p lang gezogen
(pizz.)

170
K
Hrn. 1
in F
I.
dimin.
pp
Viol. 1
Viol. 2
Vla.
Vc.
Kb.
divisi
dimin.
p
mf
pp
lang gezogen
gezogen
ppp
dim.
f
pp dimin.
pp cresc.
180
Klar. 2
in B
II.
p legato sempre
ppp

L
190
M
1. Fl. 2.
Ob. 1. 2
1. in B Klar. 2. in B
Fag. 1. 2
1. 2. in F Hrn. 3. 4. in F
A. T. Pos. B.
B.-Tuba
Viol. 1
Viol. 2
Vla.
Vc.
Kb
I. (=III.)
II. (=IV.)
sine Sordini
arco
(divisi)
pizz.
legato
(p) poco a poco cresc.
poco a poco cresc.
a 2

200
N
1.
Fl.
2.
Ob.1.2
1. in B
Klar.
2. in B
Fag.1.2
1.2. in F
Hrn.
3.4. in F
1.2. in F
Tromp.
3. in F
A.T.
Pos.
B.
B.-Tuba
Viol. 1
Viol. 2
Vla.
Vc.
Kb.
cresc.
(mf) cresc.
(a 2)
a 2
ff
cresc. sempre
(cresc. sempre)
arco
N
200

1.
Fl.
2.
p doch hervortretend
p doch hervortretend
Ob. 1. 2
(a 2)
pp
1. in B
Klar.
2. in B
p doch hervortretend
p doch hervortretend
Fag. 1. 2
a 2
1. 2. in F
Hrn.
3. 4. in F
1. 2. in F
Tromp.
3. in F
(a 2)
A. T.
Pos.
B.
(a 2)
B.-Tuba
sempre dimin.
Viol. 1
dim.
pp
Viol. 2
divisi sempre
dim.
pp
Vla.
pizz.
dim.
p
Vc.
dim.
Kb.
dim.

210
O
1.
Fl.
2.
Ob. 1.2
a 2
cresc.
1. in B
Klar.
2. in B
Tromp. 1 in F
I.
(p) poco a poco cresc.
p poco a poco cresc.
p
cresc.
Viol. 1
Viol. 2
Vla.
poco a poco cresc.
1.2. in F
Hrn.
3.4. in F
(mf) I.
2. in F
Tromp.
3. in F
II.
mf
(f) cresc. sempre
(f)
Vc.
pizz.

1.
Fl.
2.
Ob. 1.2
(a 2)
1. in B
Klar.
2. in B
Fag. 1.2
a 2
(cresc.)
1.2. in F
Hrn.
3.4. in F
marc.
a 2
ff marc. sempre
1.2. in F
Tromp.
3. in F
A. T.
Pos.
B.
B.-Tuba
Viol. 1
Viol. 2
Vla.
(arco)
Vc.
arco
Kb.
ff marcato sempre

220
P (Langsamer)
1.
Fl.
2.
Ob. 1. 2
1. in B
Klar.
2. in B
Fag. 1. 2
1. 2. in F
Hrn.
3. 4. in F
1. 2. in F
Tromp.
3. in F
A. T.
Pos.
B.
B.-Tuba
Pk.
Viol. 1
Viol. 2
Vla.
Vc.
Kb.
(a 2)
a 2
fff
fff marc. sempre
(divisi)
P (Langsamer)
220
P Langsamer

1.
Fl.
2.
Ob. 1. 2
1. in B
Klar.
2. in B
Fag. 1. 2
a 2
(a 2)
1.2. in F
Hrn.
3.4. in F
(a 2)
1.2. in F
Tromp.
3. in F
a 2
A.T.
Pos.
B.
B.-Tuba
Pk.
Viol. 1
Viol. 2
Vla.
Vc.
Kb.

1.
Fl.
2.
Ob. 1. 2
(a 2)
1. in B
Klar.
2. in B
Fag. 1. 2
1. 2. in F
Hrn.
3. 4. in F
1. 2. in F
Tromp.
3. in F
A. T.
Pos.
B.
B.-Tuba
Viol. 1
Viol. 2
Vla.
Vc.
Kb.

230
Fl.
1.
2.
Ob. 1. 2
Klar.
1. in B
2. in B
Fag. 1. 2
Hrn.
1. 2. in F
3. 4. in F
Tromp.
1. 2. in F
3. in F
Pos.
A. T.
B.
B.-Tuba
Pk.
Viol. 1
Viol. 2
Vla.
Vc.
Kb.
p
dimin.
(a 2)
pp
ppp
230

* (Klammern Bruckners)

III: SCHERZO

Bewegt
1. Flöten 2.
Oboen 1. 2
1. in B Klarinetten 2. in B
Fagotte 1. 2
1. 2. in F Hörner 3. 4. in F
1. 2. in F Trompeten 3. in F
Alt, Tenor Posaunen Baß
Baß-Tuba
Pauken B-F
a 2
semp.
(Bewegt)
Die Viertelnote im Jagdthema immer etwas länger
Violine 1
Violine 2
Viola
Violoncell
Kontrabaß
(Bewegt)

10
1. Fl. 2.
Ob.1.2
1.in B Klar. 2.in B
Fag.1.2
1.2.in F Hrn. 3.4.in F
(a 2)
1.2.in F Tromp. 3.in F
II.
I.
A.T. Pos. B.
B.-Tuba
Pk.
Viol.1
(divisi)
Viol.2
(divisi)
Vla.
(divisi)
Vc.
Kb.
10

A
20
1.
Fl.
2.
poco a poco cresc.
sempre ff
Ob.1.2
1.in B
Klar.
2.in B
Fag.1.2
pp poco a poco cresc.
1.2.in F
Hrn.
3.4.in F
a 2
ff
1.2.in F
Tromp.
3.in F
A.T.
Pos.
B.
B.-Tuba
Pk.
Viol.1
Viol.2
Vla.
Vc.
Kb.
ff sempre

30
B
1.
Fl.
2.
Ob.1.2
1.in B
Klar.
2.in B
1.2.in F
Hrn.
3.4.in F
1.2.in F
Tromp.
3.in F
A.T.
Pos.
B.
B.-Tuba
Viol.1
Viol.2
Vla.
Vc.
Kb.
a 2
(a 2)
ff
semp. ff
mf
divisi
p
pp
40
Fl.1
Hrn.
1.2.in F
I.
cresc.
mf cresc. semp.
p cresc. semp.
f
pizz.
dimin.
pp

50
C
Fl.1
1.in B
Klar.
2.in B
Hrn.
1.2.in F
Tromp.1
in F
Viol.1
Viol.2
Vla.
Vc.
Kb.
dimin.
pp
ppp
(dimin.)
(ppp)
D
60
Ob.1
divisi
cresc.
ppp cresc.
pp spicc. semp.
poco a poco cresc.

70
1.
Fl.
2.
I.
mf
cresc.
f
ff
Ob.1.2
a 2
mf
f
cresc.
ff
1.in B
Klar.
2.in B
mf
f
cresc.
ff
Fag.1.2
ff
1.2.in F
Hrn.
3.4.in F
(a 2)
(f)
a 2
mf
(f)
ff
1.2.in F
Tromp.
3.in F
a 2
ff
A.T.
Pos.
B.
ff
B.-Tuba
ff
Viol.1
(divisi)
Viol.2
ff (divisi)
Vla.
ff (divisi)
Vc.
arco
ff
Kb.
arco
ff
70

1.
Fl.
2.
Ob.1.2
1.in B
Klar.
2.in B
Fag.1.2
(a 2)
1.2.in F
Hrn.
3.4.in F
(a 2)
1.2.in F
Tromp.
3.in F
A.T.
Pos.
B.
B.-Tuba
Viol.1
Viol.2
Vla.
Vc.
Kb.

80
1.
Fl.
2.
Ob.1.2
1.in B
Klar.
2.in B
Fag.1.2
1.2.in F
Hrn.
3.4.in F
a 2
a 2
1.2.in F
Tromp.
3.in F
A.T.
Pos.
B.
B.-Tuba
Pk.
(ff)
Viol.1
Viol.2
Vla.
Vc.
Kb.
80

90
E Etwas langsamer
I.
1.
Fl.
2.
Ob.1.2
1.in B
Klar.
2.in B
Fag.1.2
(a 2)
1.2.in F
Hrn.
3.4.in F
1.2.in F
Tromp.
3.in F
A.T.
Pos.
B.
B.-Tuba
Pk.
E (Etwas langsamer)
Viol.1
Viol.2
Vla.
Vc.
Kb.
(div.)
ppp
90
E Etwas langsamer

100
110
1. Fl. 2.
Ob.1.2
1.in B Klar. 2.in B
Fag.1.2
Hrn.1 in F
Tromp.1 in F
Viol.1.
Viol.2.
Vla.
Vc.
Kb.
cresc. semp.
cresc.
F
Etwas ruhiger
120
Ob 1.
Klar.1 in B
Hrn. 1.2. in F
pizz.
(Etwas ruhiger)

Klar.1 in B
A.T. Pos. B.
Viol.2
Vla.
Vc.
Kb.
I.
p
mf
dimin. semp.
ppp
(arco)
mf lang gezogen
divisi
pizz.
pp
130
G
Fl.1
Fag.1
Hrn.1. in F
(ppp)
Ob.1.2
Tromp.1 in F
Viol.1
140
stringendo
1. spicc.
2. pizz.
cresc. poco a poco

150
Tempo Imo
Fl.1
Ob.1.2
a 2
mf
f marc.
cresc.
1. in B
Klar.
2. in B
Hrn.1
in F
Tromp.1
in F
I.
ppp
pp
(Tempo I)
4tel Note im Jagdthema länger
arco
Viol.1
Viol.2
Vla.
Vc.
Kb.
cresc. semp.
(mf)
(f)
160
H
1.
Fl.
2.
Klar.1
in B
1.2.in F
Hrn.
3.4.in F
p
Viol. 2
pp

170
1. Fl. 2.
Ob.1.2
1.in B Klar. 2.in B
Fag.1.2
1.2.in F Hrn. 3.4.in F
(a 2)
1.2.in F Tromp. 3.in F
II. p
A.T. Pos. B.
B.-Tuba
Pk.
Viol.1
Viol.2
Vla.
Vc.
Kb.
pp
p
divisi
170

180
1.
Fl.
2.
Ob.1.2
1.in B
Klar.
2.in B
Fag.
1.2.in F
Hrn.
3.4.in F
1.2.in F
Tromp.
3.in F
A.T.
Pos.
B.
B.-Tuba
Pk.
Viol.1
Viol.2
Vla.
Vc.
Kb.
cresc. semp.
ff
ff stacc. semp.
(I.)
(II.)
(ff)
arco
180

190
1. Fl. 2.
Ob.1.2
1.in B Klar. 2.in B
Fag.1.2
1.2.in F Hrn. 3.4.in F
1.2.in F Tromp. 3.in F
A.T. Pos. B.
B.-Tuba
Pk.
Viol.1
Viol.2
Vla.
Vc.
Kb.
a 2
ff
stacc. semp.
190

K
200
I.
1.
Fl.
2.
ff
pp
Ob.1.2
1. in B
Klar.
2. in B
(a 2)
1.2. in F
Hrn.
3.4. in F
ppp
(ppp)
1.2. in F
Tromp.
3. in F
A.T.
Pos.
B.
B.-Tuba
Viol.1
Viol.2
Vla.
dimin.
Vc.
Kb.

(I.)
Fl.1
Ob.1.2
mf
1.in B
Klar.
2.in B
I.
Fag.1
Hrn.1
in F
pp
Viol.1
Viol.2
Vla.
Vc.
Kb.
210
ppp
pizz.
arco
L
1.
Fl.
2.
Klar.1
in B
1.in F
Hrn.
3.4. in F
I.(=III.)
Viertelnote länger
II. (=IV.)
(ppp)

M
220
I.
Fl.1
Klar.
1 in B
spicc. semp.
Viol.1
Viol.2
divisi
spicc. semp.
Vla.
Vc.
Kb.
230
N
1.
Fl.
2.
a 2
cresc.
Ob.1.2
1.in B
Klar.
2.in B
Fag.1.2
cresc. semp.
1.2.in F
Hrn.
3.4.in F
1.2.in F
Tromp.
3. in F
Pk.
poco a poco cresc.
arco

240

1. Fl. 2.

(a 2)

Ob. 1.2

1. in B Klar. 2. in B

a 2

Fag. 1.2

(a 2)

1.2. in F Hrn. 3.4. in F

a 2

(a 2)

1.2. in F Tromp. 3. in F

A.T. Pos. B.

B.-Tuba

Pk.

Viol. 1

Viol. 2

Vla.

Vc.

Kb.

240

250
1.
Fl.
2.
Ob. 1.2
1. in B
Klar.
2. in B
(a 2)
Fag. 1.2
1.2. in F
Hrn.
(a 2)
3.4. in F
a 2
1.2. in F
Tromp.
3. in F
A. T.
Pos.
B.
B.-Tuba
Pk.
Viol. 1
Viol. 2
Vla.
Vc.
Kb.
250

1.
Fl.
2.
Ob. 1.2
1. in B
Klar.
2. in B
Fag. 1.2
a 2
1.2. in F
Hrn.
3.4. in F
1.2. in F
Tromp.
3. in F
A.T.
Pos.
B.
B. Tub
Pk.
Viol. 1
Viol. 2
Vla.
Vc.
Kb.

TRIO
Nicht zu schnell. Keinesfalls schleppend
Fl. 1.2
Ob. 1
Klar. 1 in B
p dolce
cresc.
(Nicht zu schnell. Keinesfalls schleppend)
Streicher geteilt: a arco b pizz.
Viol. 1
Viol. 2
Vla.
Vc.
pizz.
arco
pp
10
A
20
30
mf
f
ppp

B
40
1.
Fl.
2.
Ob. 1
1. in B
Klar.
2. in B
Viol. 1
Viol. 2
Vla.
Vc.
pp
ppp
cresc.
pizz.
C
50
Fl. 1
Ob. 1
Klar. 1 in B
Tromp. 1.2 in F
dimin.
a arco
b pizz.
Scherzo
da capo

IV: FINALE

Bewegt, doch nicht zu schnell
1. Flöten 2.
Oboen 1.2
1. in B Klarinetten 2. in B
Fagotte 1.2
1.2. in F Hörner 3.4. in F
1.2. in F Trompeten 3. in F
Alt, Tenor Posaunen Baß
Baß-Tuba
Pauken B-Es und C-F tief
(Bewegt, doch nicht zu schnell)
Violine 1
Violine 2
Viola
Violoncell
Kontrabaß
(Bewegt, doch nicht zu schnell)

10
1. in B
Klar.
2. in B
Hrn.
1 in F
Viol. 1
Viol. 2
Vla.
Vc.
Kb.
10
20
1.
Fl.
2.
1. in B
Klar.
2. in B
Hrn.
1 in F
Tromp.
1 in F
Viol. 1
Viol. 2
Vla.
Vc.
Kb.
cresc.
p
I. semp.
divisi
pp
20

1.
Fl.
2.
Ob. 1. 2
1. in B
Klar.
2. in B
Tromp. 1
in F
Viol. 1
Viol. 2
Vla.
Vc.
Kb.
(I.)
a 2 semp.
p
poco a poco crescendo
30
Hrn.
1. 2. in F
3. in F
Tromp. 3
in F
I. (=III.)
cresc. semp.
(III.)
f
mf

40
1.
Fl.
2.
f cresc. semp.
f cresc. semp.
(a 2)
Ob. 1. 2
f cresc. semp.
1. in B
Klar.
2. in B
f cresc. semp.
f cresc. semp.
Fag. 1. 2
f
cresc. semp.
1. 2. in F
Hrn.
3. 4. in F
f
cresc. semp.
cresc. semp.
1. 2. in F
Tromp.
3. in F
I.
II.
(f)
f
cresc. semp.
cresc. semp.
(f)
A. T.
Pos.
B.
mf cresc. semp.
mf cresc. semp.
f
f
Pk.
ff
Viol. 1
cresc. semp.
Viol. 2
cresc. semp.
Vla.
cresc. semp.
Vc.
cresc. semp.
Kb.
cresc. semp.
40

Langsamer
A
50
1.
Fl.
2.
Ob. 1. 2
1. in B
Klar.
2. in B
Fag. 1. 2
1. 2. in F
Hrn.
3. 4. in F
1. 2. in F
Tromp.
3. in F
A. T.
Pos.
B.
B.-Tuba
Pk.
Viol. 1
Viol. 2
Vla.
Vc.
Kb.
(Langsamer)
ff
(ff)
a 2
(a 2)
marc. semp.
marc.
Langsamer

1.
Fl.
2.
Ob. 1. 2
1. in B
Klar.
2. in B
Fag. 1. 2
1. 2. in F
Hrn.
3. 4. in F
1. 2. in F
Tromp.
3. in F
A. T.
Pos.
B.
B.-Tuba
Viol. 1
Viol. 2
Vla.
Vc.
Kb.
(a 2)
dimin.
dim.
pp

60
1. Fl. 2.
Klar. 1 in B
1.2. in F Hrn. 3.4. in F
(a 2)
Tromp. 1 in F
Viol. 1
Viol. 2
Vla.
Vc.
Kb.
p poco a poco crescendo
p poco a poco cresc.
poco a poco crescendo
Ob. 1.2
1. in B Klar. 2. in B
Fag. 1.2
1.2. in F Tromp. 3. in F
A.T. Pos. B.
f marcato semp.
f marc. semp.
f marc.
cresc.
ff marc.
(divisi)

70
1.
Fl.
2.
ff marc. semp.
fff marc. semp.
(a 2)
Ob.1.2
fff marcato semp.
1.in B
Klar.
2.in B
fff marcato semp.
a 2
Fag.1.2
ff
1.2.in F
Hrn.
3.4.in F
ff marc.
fff marc. semp.
1.2.in F
Tromp.
3.in F
A.T.
Pos.
B.
B.-Tuba
fff
Viol.1
Viol.2
(divisi)
Vla.
Vc.
Kb.
70

80
1.
Fl.
2.
marc. semp.
(a 2)
Ob.1.2
1. in B
Klar.
2. in B
Fag.1.2
marc.
1.2. in F
Hrn.
3.4. in F
1.2. in F
Tromp.
3. in F
A.T.
Pos.
B.
B.-Tuba
Pk.
fff
Viol.1
(divisi)
Viol.2
divisi
Vla.
Vc.
Kb.
80

90
1. Fl. 2.
Ob.1.2
1.in B Klar. 2.in B
Fag.1.2
1.2.in F Hrn. 3.4.in F
dimin. semp.
pp dimin.
1.2.in F Tromp. 3.in F
A.T. Pos. B.
B.-Tuba
Pk.
dimin. semp.
pp dimin.
ppp
Viol.1
Viol.2
dimin. semp.
pp
Vla.
(dimin. semp.)
pp
Vc.
Kb.
90
B Noch langsamer
Muta in C, F
Pk.
B Noch langsamer
Viol.1
p
cresc.
pp
Viol.2
pp
dim.
pp
Vla.
lang gezogen
p immer hervortretend
cresc.
pp
pizz.
Vc.
pp
pizz.
Kb.
pp
B Noch langsamer

100
ritard.
Fl.1
Ob.1
Klar.1 in B
Viol.1
Viol.2
Vla.
Vc.
Kb.
cresc.
mf
p
dimin.
pp
(ritard.)
C a Tempo
110
I.
semp. pizz.
(pp)
Hrn.1 in F
ppp cresc.
p cresc.
mf cresc.
ppp (cresc.)
(p)

120
1. Fl. 2.
Ob.1.2
Klar.1 in B
1.2.in F Hrn. 3.4.in F
Viol.1
Viol.2
Vla.
Vc.
Kb.
p
cresc.
I.
(I.)
mf
pp
(pp) cresc.
f
dimin.
D
130
Fl 1
Ob 1
Klar.1 in B
Fag.1.2
1.in F Hrn. 3.in F
Tromp.1 in F
I.semp.
(mf)
I. (=III.)
(cresc.)
arco
pizz.
p doch immer herwortretend

Fl.1
Ob.1
Klar.1 in B
1.2.in F
Hrn.
3.4.in F
Viol.1
Viol.2
Vla.
Vc.
Kb.
p dimin.
p dim.
cresc.
140
1. Fl. 2.
Ob.1.2
1.in B Klar. 2.in B
1.2.in F Tromp. 3.in F
A.T. Pos. B.
B.-Tuba
Pk.
pizz.

1.
Fl.
2.
Ob.1.2
1.in B
Klar.
2.in B
1.in F
Hrn.
3.4.in F
1.2.in F
Tromp.
3.in F
A.T.
Pos.
B.
B.-Tuba
Pk.
Viol.1
Viol.2
Vla.
Vc.
Kb.
cresc.
Muta C in B
gezogen
pizz.
div.
150
Ob.1
Hrn.
3.4 in F

E
1.
Fl.
2
Ob. 1.2
1. in B
Klar.
2. in B
Fag. 1.2
a 2
1.2. in F
Hrn.
3.4. in F
ff marc. semp.
1.2. in F
Tromp.
3. in F
A. T.
Pos.
Pk.
gestrichen
Viol. 1
ff marcato semp
Viol. 2
ff marc. semp.
Vla.
arco
Vc.
Kb.
ff marcato semp.

160
1.
Fl.
2.
a 2
Ob. 1.2
1. in B
Klar.
2. in B
Fag. 1.2
(a 2)
1.2. in F
Hrn.
3.4. in F
1.2. in F
Tromp.
3. in F
marcato
A.T.
Pos.
B.
marc.
Pk.
Viol. 1
Viol. 2
Vla.
Vc.
Kb
160

1.
Fl.
2.
Ob. 1. 2
1. in B
Klar.
2. in B
Fag. 1. 2
(a 2)
1. 2. in F
Hrn.
3. 4. in F
1. 2. in F
Tromp.
3. in F
a 2
A. T.
Pos.
B.
B.-Tuba
Pk.
Viol. 1
Viol. 2
Vla.
Vc.
Kb.

170
1. Fl. 2.
Ob. 1.2
1. in B Klar. 2. in B
Fag. 1.2
1.2. in F Hrn. 3.4. in F
1.2. in F Tromp. 3. in F
A. T. Pos. B.
B.-Tuba
Pk.
Viol. 1
Viol. 2
Vla.
Vc.
Kb.
marc.
(a 2)
170

1.
Fl.
2.
(a 2)
Ob. 1.2
1. in B
Klar.
2. in B
Fag. 1.2
a 2
1.2. in F
Hrn.
3.4. in F
1.2. in F
Tromp.
3. in F
A. T.
Pos.
B.
B.-Tuba
Muta in Es B
Pk.
Viol. 1
Viol. 2
Vla.
Vc.
Kb.

180
F poco a poco ritard.
1.
Fl.
2.
Ob. 1.2
1. in B
Klar.
2. in B
Fag. 1.2
1.2. in F
Hrn.
3.4. in F
1.2. in F
Tromp.
3. in F
A. T.
Pos.
B.
B.-Tuba
F poco a poco ritard.
Viol. 1
Viol. 2
Vla.
Vc.
Kb.
180
F poco a poco ritard.

Langsam
190
Fag. 1.2
Hrn. 3 in F
I. (=III)
p
cresc.
dim.
cresc.
(Langsam)
Viol. 1
p
Viol. 2
divisi
pp
hervortretend
Vla.
p
cresc.
dim.
cresc.
Vc.
p
Kb.
pizz.
pp
Langsam
190
Klar. 1 in B
I.
p
dim.
Fag. 1.2
Hrn. 3 in F
mf
cresc.
p
dim.
pp
A. T.
Pos.
B.
pp
ppp
dim.
pp
ppp
dim.
Viol. 1
cresc.
pp
dim.
Viol. 2
pp
dim.
Vla.
mf
cresc.
p
pp
Vc.
cresc.
(pp)
Kb.
cresc.
pp

200
G Tempo wie anfangs
1. Fl. 2.
1. in B Klar. 2. in B
Hrn. 3 in F
A. T. Pos. B.
G (Tempo wie anfangs)
Viol. 1
Viol. 2
Vla.
Vc.
pizz.
Kb.
pizz.
200
G Tempo wie anfangs
210
Klar. 1 in B
Fag. 1
Hrn. 1 in F
Viol. 1
Viol. 2
Vla.
Vc.
Kb.
210

1.in B
Klar.
2.in B
pp poco a poco cresc.
p cresc.
Fag.1
poco a poco cresc.
I.
Hrn.1
in F
Viol.1
Viol.2
Vla.
Vc.
Kb.
220
(cresc.)
mf
f
(I.)
p
1.in F
Hrn.
3.in F
I. (=III)
Tromp.3
in F
(III.)
cresc. semp.

230
1. Fl. 2.
Ob.1.2
1.in B Klar. 2.in B
Hrn. 3.4.in F
Tromp.3 in F
I.(=III.)
(III.)
(IV.)
Viol.1
Viol.2
Vla.
Vc.
Kb.
pizz.
semp. pizz.
mf (cresc.)
cresc.
crescendo
230
H
240
1.2.in F Hrn. 3.4.in F
a 2
A.T. Pos. B.
B.-Tuba
semp. dim.
H
240

Fl.1
hervortretend
250
I.
mf
cresc.
1.2. in F
Hrn.
3.4. in F
(a 2)
f dim.
pp
A.T.
Pos.
B.
B.-Tuba
Viol.1
G Saite
arco
ff
lang gezogen
p
Viol.2
gezogen
Vla.
divisi
Vc.
(divisi)
Kb.
(I.)
Klar.1 in B
Hrn.1 in F
cresc. semp.
pp
p cresc.
p (cresc.)
mf cresc.
lang gezogen
f cresc.

*) (Klammern Bruckners)

280
Ob.1
Klar.1 in B
1.in F
Hrn.
3.in F
Viol.1
Viol.2
Vla.
Vc.
Kb.
I.
I.(=III.)
arco
mf
p
pp
cresc.
dim.
280
Ob.1
Fag.1
Viol.1
Viol.2
Vla.
Vc.
Kb.
Triolen: lang und breit gestrichen hier
lang gestrichen immer
lang gestrichen immer
lang gestrichen immer
f
dim.
L
290
Viol.1
Viol.2
Vla.
Vc.
Kb.
ppp
290

M
1.
Fl.
2.
Ob.1.2
1.in B
Klar.
2.in B
Fag.1.2
a 2 semp.
1.2.in F
Hrn.
3.4.in F
a 2
1.2.in F
Tromp.
3.in F
a 2
A.T.
Pos.
B.
B.-Tuba
M
Viol.1
fff markiert gestrichen immer fort
Viol.2
fff markiert gestrichen
Vla.
fff markiert gestrichen
Vc.
fff markiert gestrichen
Kb.
fff markiert gestrichen immer fort
M

300
1.
Fl.
2.
Ob.1.2
1.in B
Klar.
2.in B
(a 2)
Fag.1.2
1.2.in F
Hrn.
3.4.in F
(a 2)
1.2.in F
Tromp.
3.in F
(a 2)
A.T.
Pos.
B.
B-Tuba
Viol.1
Viol.2
Vla.
Vc.
Kb.
300

1.
Fl.
2.
Ob.1.2
1.in B
Klar.
2.in B
(a 2)
Fag.1.2
1.2.in F
Hrn.
3.4.in F
(a 2)
1.2.in F
Tromp.
3.in F
A.T.
Pos.
B.
B.-Tuba
Viol.1
Viol.2
Vla.
Vc.
Kb.

310
1.
Fl.
2.
Ob.1.2
a 2
1.in B
Klar.
2.in B
(a 2)
Fag.1.2
1.2.in F
Hrn.
3.4.in F
1.2.in F
Tromp.
3.in F
marc. semp.
A.T.
Pos.
B.
B.-Tuba
Viol.1
Viol.2
Vla.
Vc.
Kb.
310

1.
Fl.
2.
Ob. 1.2
a 2
1. in B
Klar.
2. in B
Fag. 1.2
(a 2)
1.2. in F
Hrn.
3.4. in F
(a 2)
1.2. in F
Tromp.
3. in F
marc.
A.T.
Pos.
B.
B.-Tuba
Viol. 1
Viol. 2
Vla.
Vc.
Kb.

320
N
1.
Fl.
2.
a 2
Ob.1.2
1.in B
Klar.
2.in B
(a 2)
Fag.1.2
a 2 semp.
1.2. in F
Hrn.
3.4.in F
1.2.in F
Tromp.
3.in F
A.T.
Pos.
B.
B.-Tuba
Viol.1
Viol.2
Vla.
Vc.
Kb.

1.
Fl.
2.
Ob.1.2
1.in B
Klar.
2.in B
Fag.1.2
1.2.in F
Hrn.
3.4.in F
1.2.in F
Tromp.
3.in F
A.T.
Pos.
B.
B.-Tuba
Viol.1
Viol.2
Vla.
Vc.
Kb.
(a 2)
marc. semp.

330
1.
Fl.
2.
(a 2)
Ob.1.2
1.in B
Klar.
2.in B
Fag.1.2
1.2.in F
Hrn.
3.4.in F
marc. semp.
(a 2)
1.2.in F
Tromp.
3.in F
a 2
A.T.
Pos.
B.
B.-Tuba
Viol.1
Viol.2
Vla.
Vc.
Kb.
330

ritard.
1.
Fl.
2.
(a 2)
Ob.1.2
1.in B
Klar.
2.in B
Fag.1.2
1.2.in F
Hrn.
3.4.in F
(a 2)
I.(dim. semp.)
1.2.in F
Tromp.
3.in F
A.T.
Pos.
B.
dim. semp.
dim. semp.
B.-Tuba
dim. semp.
ritard.
Viol.1
dim. semp.
Viol.2
dim. semp.
Vla.
dim. semp.
Vc.
dim. semp.
Kb.
dim. semp.
ritard.

Klar. 2 in B
Fag. 1.2
1.2. in F
Hrn.
3.4. in F
Viol. 1
Vla.
Vc.
Kb.
340
(p)
(dim.)
p
dim.
p lang gezogen
II.
semp. pp
pp lang gezogen
Fl. 1
Ob. 1
Klar. 1 in B
Pk.
350
cresc.
dim.
I. (=III.)
ppp
pizz.

*) (Klammern Bruckners)

*) (Klammern Bruckners)

400
1. Fl. 2.
Ob.1.2
(a 2)
1.in B Klar. 2.in B
Fag.1.2
1.2.in F Hrn. 3.4.in F
1.2.in F Tromp. 3.in F
A.T. Pos. B.
B.-Tuba
Viol.1
Viol.2
Vla.
Vc.
Kb.
400

Langsamer
1.
Fl.
2.
(a 2)
Ob.1.2
1. in B
Klar.
2. in B
(a 2)
Fag.1.2
(a 2)
1.2. in F
Hrn.
3.4. in F
1.2. in F
Tromp.
3. in F
A.T.
Pos.
B.
B.-Tuba
(Langsamer)
Viol.1
divisi
Viol.2
Vla.
Vc.
Kb.
(Langsamer)

410
1.
Fl.
2.
a 2
Ob.1.2
1.in B
Klar.
2.in B
Fag.1.2
1.2.in F
Hrn.
3.4.in F
1.2.in F
Tromp.
3.in F
A.T.
Pos.
B.
B.-Tuba
Viol.1
Viol.2
Vla.
Vc.
Kb.
I.
p
pp
lang gezogen
hervortretend
pizz.
410

Fl.1
Kl.ar.1 in B
Viol.1
Viol.2
Vla.
Vc.
Kb.
420
Hrn.1 in F
getragen
pp legato
R
arco
gezogen
1. in F
Hrn.
3.4. in F
I. (=III.)
II. (=IV.)
(ritard. semp.)
430
pizz.
cresc.
dim.
dimin.

S Etwas bewegter
1.
Fl.
2.
Ob.1.2
1.in B
Klar.
2.in B
1.2.in F
Hrn.
3.in F
I. (=III.)
S (Etwas bewegter)
Viol.1
Viol.2
Vla.
Vc.
Kb.
pizz.
S (Etwas bewegter)
440
Klar.1 in B
cresc.
dimin.
dim.
pp poco a poco cresc.
440

Ob.1.2
1.in B
Klar.
2.in B
Viol.1
Viol.2
Vla.
Vc.
Kb.
pp
T
450
a 2
Fag.1.2
1.in F
Hrn.
4.in F
I.
II. (=IV.)
divisi
arco
pizz.
cresc.
f
(f)

460
1.
Fl.
2.
Ob.1.2
(a 2)
1.in B
Klar.
2.in B
Fag.1.2
1.2.in F
Hrn.
3.4.in F
I.
II.(=IV.)
a 2
1.2.in F
Tromp.
3.in F
A.T.
Pos.
B.
Viol.1
Viol.2
Vla.
Vc.
Kb.
dim.
dimin.
p
pp
cresc.
(cresc.)
p cresc.
460

1.
Fl.
2.
Ob.1.2
1.in B
Klar.
2.in B
Fag.1.2
1.2.in F
Hrn.
3.4.in F
1.2.in F
Tromp.
3.in F
A.T.
Pos.
B.
B.-Tuba
Pk.
Viol.1
Viol.2
Vla.
Vc.
Kb.
Langsam
(Langsam)
(a 2)
arco
gezogen
pp hervortretend
f
ff
ppp
pp

470
ritard.
1. Fl. 2.
1. in B Klar. 2. in B
Hrn. 3.4. in F
ppp semp.
Pk.
ppp semp.
(ritard.)
Viol. 1
Viol. 2
Vla.
dim.
Vc.
ppp
Kb.
ppp
470
(ritard.)
Tempo I^mo
480
Ob. 1
pp semp.
Klar. 1 in B
pp semp.
Fag. 1
pp semp.
Hrn. 1 in F
pp semp.
(Tempo I)
Viol. 1
ppp
Viol. 2
ppp
Vla.
ppp
Vc.
ppp
Kb.
ppp
480
(Tempo I)

490
Ob.1
Klar.1 in B
Fag.1
1.in F
Hrn.
3.4.in F
A.T.
Pos.
B.
Viol.1
Viol.2
Vla.
Vc.
Kb.
pp
490
500
crescendo
etwas hervortretend
500

W
1.
Fl.
2.
Ob.1.2
1.in B
Klar.
2.in B
Fag.1.2
1.2.in F
Hrn.
3.4.in F
Tromp. 1.2.in F
A.T.
Pos.
B.
B.-Tuba
Pk.
Viol.1
Viol.2
Vla.
Vc.
Kb.
I.
dim.
a 2
p
pp

510
1. Fl. 2.
mf cresc.
f cresc.
Ob.1.2
f (cresc.)
1.in B Klar. 2.in B
Fag.1.2
a 2
1.2.in F Hrn. 3.4.in F
Tromp. 1.2 in F
dimin.
B.-Tuba
p cresc.
Pk.
p cresc. semp.
Viol.1
Viol.2
Vla.
Vc.
Kb.
mf cresc.
dim.
X
520
2.in F Hrn. 4.in F
II.
p poco a poco cresc.
II. (=IV.)
p (poco a poco cresc.)
1.2.in F Tromp. 3.in F
pp
A.T. Pos. B.
pp poco a poco cresc.
cresc.

530
Y
1.
Fl.
2.
Ob.1.2
1.in B
Klar.
2.in B
Fag.1.2
2.in F
Hrn.
4.in F
1.2.in F
Tromp.
3.in F
A.T.
Pos.
B.
B.-Tuba
Viol.1
Viol.2
Vla.
Vc.
Kb.
mf cresc. semp.
mf cresc.semp.
ff
f (cresc.)
(f cresc.)
mf
cresc.
f
divisi

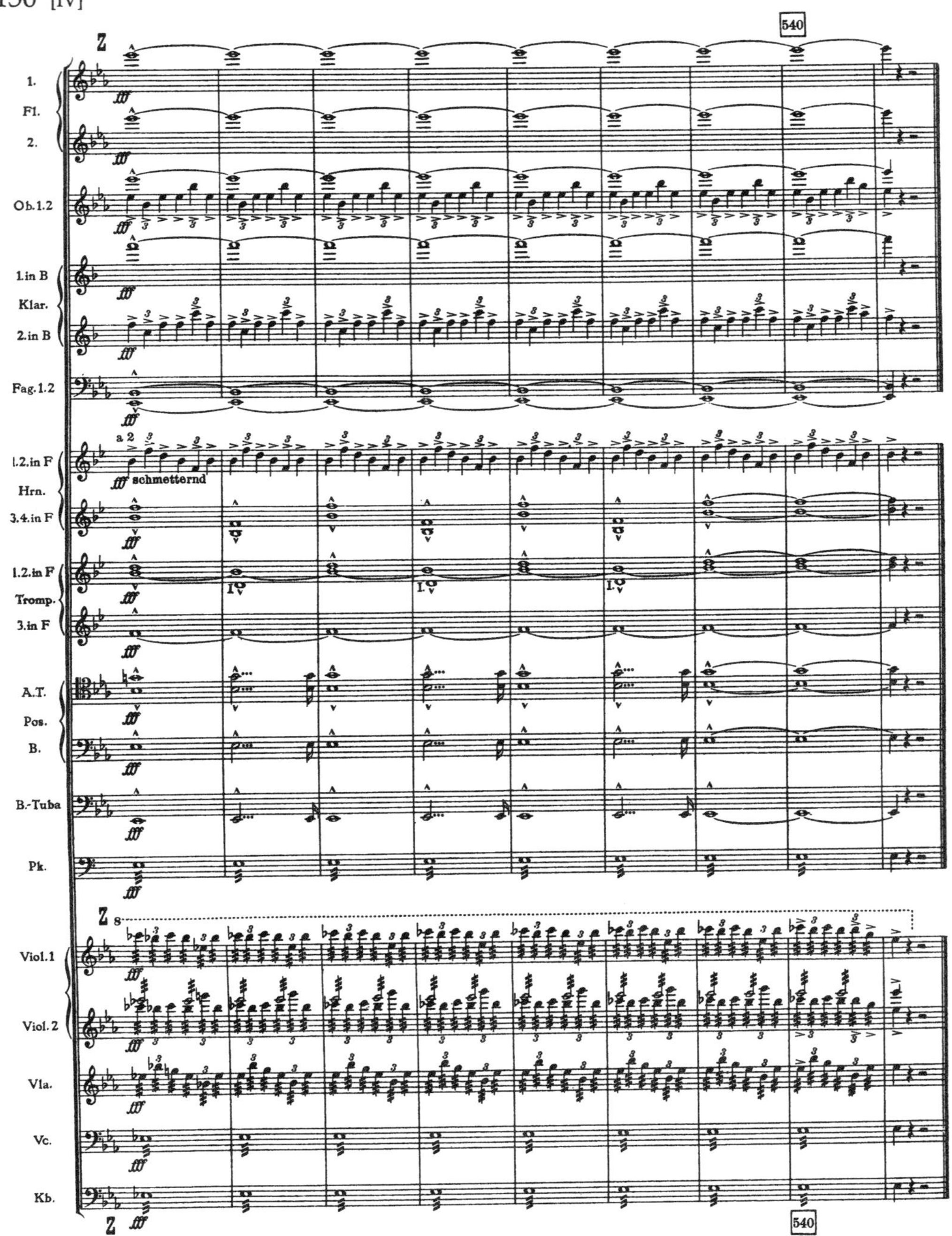
Z
540
1.
Fl.
2.
Ob.1.2
1.in B
Klar.
2.in B
Fag.1.2
a 2
schmetternd
1.2.in F
Hrn.
3.4.in F
1.2.in F
Tromp.
3.in F
A.T.
Pos.
B.
B.-Tuba
Pk.
Z
Viol.1
Viol.2
Vla.
Vc.
Kb.
Z
540